CRABTREE CONTACT

TOP 10 BIGGEST

Ben Hubbard

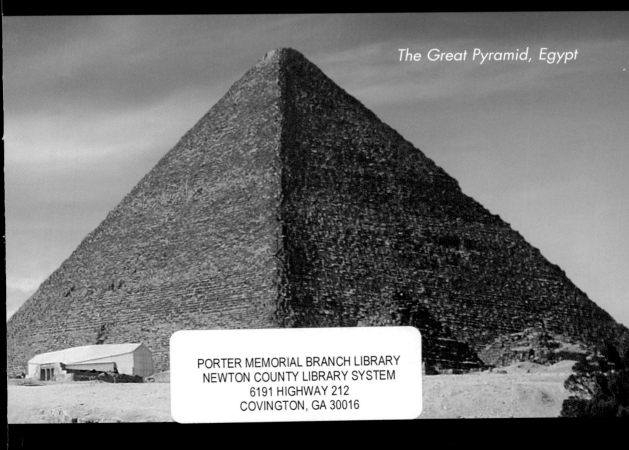

The Great Pyramid, Egypt

Crabtree Publishing Company

www.crabtreebooks.com

Crabtree Publishing Company

www.crabtreebooks.com

PMB 59051
350 Fifth Avenue, 59th Floor
New York, NY, 10118

Content development by
Shakespeare Squared

www.ShakespeareSquared.com

1-800-387-7650

616 Welland Avenue,
St. Catharines, Ontario
L2M 5V6

Published by
Crabtree Publishing
Company © 2010

First published
in Great Britain in
2010 by TickTock
Entertainment Ltd.

Printed in the
U.S.A./122009
CG20091120

Crabtree Publishing
Company credits:
Project manager: Kathy Middleton
Editor: Reagan Miller
Proofreader: Crystal Sikkens
Production coordinator: Katherine Berti
Prepress technician: Katherine Berti

TickTock credits:
Publisher: Melissa Fairley
Art director: Faith Booker
Editor: Emma Dods
Designer: Emma Randall
Production controller: Ed Green
Production manager: Suzy Kelly

Thank you to Lorraine Petersen and the members of nasen

Picture credits (t=top; b=bottom; c=centre; l=left; r=right; OFC=outside front
cover): A & J Visage/Alamy: 21. Courtesy of Mallie's Sports Bar & Grill: 4, 6–7,
7b. Crystal Lagoons: 22–23. Danita Dellmont/Alamy: 25. Jean-Paul Ferrero/
ardea.com: 16. George Hall/Corbis: 12–13. Motoring Picture Library/Alamy: 18-
19. NASA Jet Propulsion Laboratory (NASA-JPL)/courtesy of nasaimages.com:
28–29. Renaud Visage/Getty Images: 20. Dennis Scott/Corbis: OFC, 5b, 16–17.
Shutterstock: 1, 2, 14–15, 24, 26, 27 both. Solent News/Rex Features: 5t, 10–11

Every effort has been made to trace copyright holders, and we apologize in advance
for any omissions. We would be pleased to insert the appropriate acknowledgments
in any subsequent edition of this publication.

Library and Archives Canada Cataloguing in Publication

Hubbard, Ben
    Top 10 biggest / Ben Hubbard.

(Crabtree contact)
Includes index.
ISBN 978-0-7787-7487-7 (bound).--ISBN 978-0-7787-7508-9 (pbk.)

        1. Size perception--Juvenile literature. I. Title.
II. Title: Top ten biggest. III. Series: Crabtree contact

BF299.S5H82 2010   j153.7'52   C2009-906464-2

Library of Congress Cataloging-in-Publication Data

Hubbard, Ben.
    Top 10 biggest / Ben Hubbard.
        p. cm. -- (Crabtree contact)
    Includes index.
    ISBN 978-0-7787-7487-7 (reinforced lib. bdg. : alk. paper) --
ISBN 978-0-7787-7508-9 (pbk. : alk. paper)
1. Size perception--Juvenile literature. I. Title. II. Title: Top ten
biggest. III. Series.

BF299.S5H834 2010
152.14'2--dc22

                                                                    2009044257

*An African
bush elephant*

CONTENTS

Introduction . . . .

Biggest Hamburger . . . .

Biggest Food Fight . . . .

Biggest Motorbike . . . .

Biggest Aircraft . . . .

Biggest Land Animal . . . . . .

Biggest Sea Animal . . . .

Biggest Production Car . . .

Biggest Flower . . . .

Biggest Swimming Pool . . .

Biggest Tomb . . . .

Big Tombs . . . .

Conclusion . . . .

Need-to-Know Words . . . . .

Big Facts/
Find Out More Online . . . .

Index . . . .

INTRODUCTION

This book is all about the world's biggest things.

From **BIG** burgers...

...to **BIG** animals...

...to **BIG** machines...

This huge burger weighed 185 pounds (84 kilograms). The beef burger took 15 hours to cook!

The world's biggest motorbike is so huge that it can crush cars!

The blue whale is the world's biggest animal. Its tongue can weigh as much as an elephant!

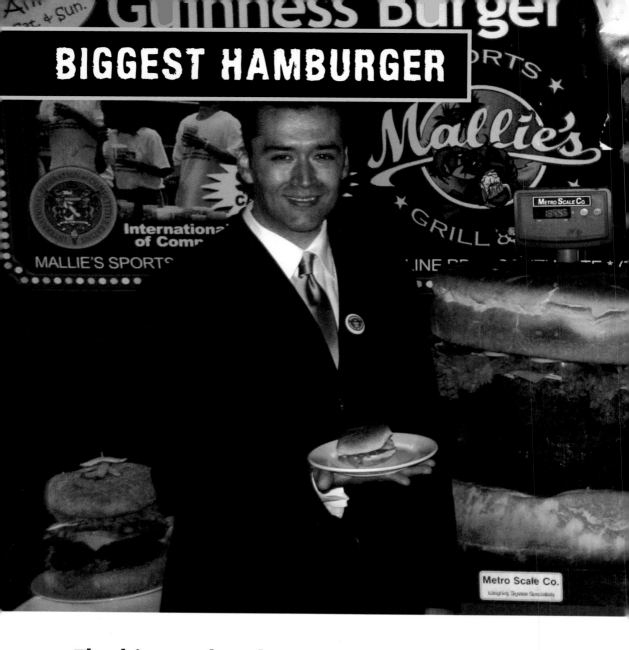

The biggest hamburger you can buy can be found at Mallie's Sports Grill & Bar, in Michigan.

The beef burger alone needed three men to carry it. After 15 hours in the oven, it was then covered with bacon, cheese, lettuce, tomatoes, onions, and pickles. After that it was put in a huge bun.

If you are interested in trying one of these "Absolutely Ridiculous Burgers," you will need to order it three days in advance.

Start saving—each burger costs around five hundred dollars!

On the last Wednesday in August, the biggest annual **food fight takes place in Buñol, Spain.**

Several large trucks transport tomatoes into town. Over 220,000 pounds (99,790 kilograms) of tomatoes are brought in for the food fight.

Tens of thousands of people from all over the world take part in the food fight.

A cannon fires to signal the start of the battle. The tomato fight lasts for exactly one hour. When the time is up, the cannon is fired again. Everyone must then stop.

Afterward, fire engine hoses are used to hose down the streets.

BIGGEST MOTORBIKE

It took retired stuntman Ray Baumann three years to build the "Monster Motorbike."

It is the biggest motorbike in the world.
The bike is nearly 30 feet (nine meters) long
and about ten feet (three meters) high.

It weighs nearly 30,000 pounds (13,608
kilograms)—that is about as heavy as a bus.

BIGGEST AIRCRAFT

The *Antonov An-225 Mriya* is the biggest aircraft in the world.

space shuttle

This is a specially built Russian **cargo** plane. It can "piggyback" big objects, including other aircraft.

Here, it is carrying the "Buran" **space shuttle** on its back.

- Length: 275 feet (84 meters)
- **Wingspan**: 290 feet (88.4 meters)
- Top speed: 528 miles per hour (850 kilometers per hour)
- Weight (when empty): 628,320 pounds (285,001 kilograms)

BIGGEST LAND ANIMAL

The African bush elephant is the biggest animal on land.

Everything about this elephant is BIG!

It can grow up to:
- 33 feet (ten meters) in length
- 13 feet (four meters) in height (to the shoulder)
- 13,230 pounds (6,001 kilograms) in weight.

Not surprisingly, African bush elephants have huge appetites. They eat up to 300 pounds (136 kilograms) of **vegetation** every day.

BIGGEST SEA ANIMAL

The blue whale is the biggest animal in the sea. It is also the biggest animal on the planet! It can weigh as much as 30 African bush elephants. Its heart alone can weigh as much as a small car!

krill

The blue whale can eat almost four tons (3.6 metric tons) of **krill** every day.

The blue whale can grow up to:
* Length: 98 feet (30 meters)
* Weight: 396,800 pounds (179,986 kilograms)

BIGGEST PRODUCTION CAR

**The Bugatti *Royale Type 41*
is the biggest production car
in the world. The car has held
this title since it was first built.**

Manufactured between 1926 and
1933, only six cars were ever built!

- Length: 22 feet (6.7 meters)
- Weight: 7,165 pounds (3,250 kilograms)

BIGGEST FLOWER

The biggest flower in the world is called *Rafflesia arnoldi.*

It is 36 inches (91 centimeters) across and can weigh up to 24 pounds (11 kilograms).

Oddly, this Southeast Asian beauty smells like rotting meat! Luckily, the flies that **pollinate** the plant love the smell.

Once it has fully developed, the flower only lives for a few days.

BIGGEST SWIMMING POOL

The San Alfonso del Mar in Chile, South America, is the biggest swimming pool in the world. It is a whopping 3,323 feet (1,013 meters) long.

The water is heated and kept at a temperature of 26°C (79°F). This allows people to enjoy the pool even on cooler days.

The pool is used for swimming, sailing, and other water sports.

Six thousand normal swimming pools can fit inside it!

The pool covers 19.7 acres (eight hectares) and holds more than 65 million gallons (246 million liters) of **filtered** seawater.

A pump sucks water in from the sea and releases it into the pool.

BIGGEST TOMB

The Great Pyramid in Egypt is the biggest tomb **on Earth.**

It was constructed 4,500 years ago from 2.3 million limestone blocks.

Each block weighs between 2.3 and 13.6 tons (2.1 and 12.3 metric tons)!

The pyramid is 453 feet (138 meters) high and covers an area of 13 acres (5.3 hectares). It took 20 years to construct.

The pyramid was built to protect Pharaoh Khufu's body and his possessions. But, tomb robbers found Khufu's burial chamber and stole its treasures.

Ivory statue of Khufu

BIG TOMBS

There are many huge tombs around the world.

The five-acre (two-hectare) burial ground of Qin Shi Huangdi, the first emperor of China, contains the Terracotta Army.

The army consists of 8,000 life-like statues of soldiers. It was believed that these soldiers would help the emperor in the afterlife.

The Taj Mahal in India was built in 1631 by the Mughal emperor, Shah Jahan, for his wife who died during childbirth. It is 240 feet (73 meters) high.

The **catacombs** of Paris in France are underground tunnels and rooms. There are 186 miles (299 kilometers) of tunnels. The catacombs contain around six million bodies.

CONCLUSION

Now you have seen ten of the biggest things in the world.

What about the biggest thing in space?

As far as we know, the biggest object in our solar system is the Sun. It is so big that you could fit one million Earths inside it.

The Sun is a burning ball of gas. We can still feel its heat from more than 93 million miles (150 million kilometers) away. Without the Sun we would freeze to death!

Sun

NEED-TO-KNOW WORDS

annual Something that occurs every year

cargo Goods carried on a ship, aircraft, or motor vehicle

catacomb An underground cemetery consisting of tunnels and empty spaces for tombs

filter A porous device for removing impurities from a liquid that is passed through it

krill Small shrimp-like marine creatures

manufacture Making things, such as cars, on a large scale using machinery

pollinate When an insect drops pollen inside a flower or plant, allowing it to produce seeds or fruit

space shuttle A reusable spacecraft with wings that carries astronauts between Earth and a space station

vegetation Plants

tomb A special building where the dead are buried

wingspan The measurement from the tip of one wing to the other

BIG FACTS

- The largest butterfly is the Queen Alexandra's Birdwing. It has a wingspan of 11 inches (28 centimeters) and is the size of a pigeon.

- The land animal with the biggest mouth is the hippopotamus. It can open its jaws to nearly 180 degrees. The average adult male hippo can open its mouth 3.9 feet (1.2 meters) wide.

FIND OUT MORE ONLINE

Bugatti
www.bugatti.com

CIA world fact book
www.cia.gov/library/publications/the-world-factbook/index.html

Guinness World Records™
www.guinnessworldrecords.com

National Geographic
www.nationalgeographic.com

Tomato Fight
www.latomatina.org

INDEX

A
aircraft 12–13
Antonov An-225 Mriya
     12–13

B
blue whales 5, 16–17
Bugatti Royale type 41 18–19
Buñol, Spain 8–9

C
catacombs 27

E
elephants 5, 14–15, 16

F
fire engines 9
flowers 20–21
food fight 8–9

G
Great Pyramid, Egypt 24–25

H
hamburgers 4, 6–7
hippopotamus 31

K
krill 16

M
motorbikes 5, 10–11

P
Pharaoh Khufu 25

Q
Qin Shi Huangdi 26
Queen Alexandra's Birdwing
     butterfly 31

R
Rafflesia arnoldi 20–21

S
San Alfonso del Mar, Chile
     22–23
Shah Jahan, Mughal emperor
     27
space 28–29
space shuttle 12–13
Sun 28–29
swimming pools 22–23

T
Taj Mahal, India 27
Terracotta Army, China
     26
tombs 24–27